Faithful Entrepreneur

The Faith & Business Series

Vanessa Miller Pierce

Vanessa Miller Pierce

vmiller01@me.com

Printed in the United States of America

© 2018 by Vanessa Miller

Praise Unlimited Enterprises

Charlotte, NC

Disclaimer

This book is designed to provide information in regard to the subject matter covered. It is sold with the understanding that the publisher and author and advisers are not rendering legal, accounting or other professional advice.

Every effort has been made to make this manual as complete and as accurate as possible. However, depending on when you are reading this book, some information may no longer be relevant. Therefore, this text should be used only as a general guide and not as the ultimate source of publishing information. Furthermore, this manual contains information only up to the date of printing.

The author, advisers and publishers shall have neither liability nor responsibility to any person or entity with respect to any loss or damage caused or alleged to be caused directly or indirectly by the information contained in this book.

Other Books by Vanessa Miller

Family Business Book I

Family Business II - Sword of Division

Family Business III - Love and Honor

Family Business IV - The Children

Family Business V - The Atonement

Sunshine and Rain

Rain in the Promised Land

After the Rain

How Sweet the Sound

Heirs of Rebellion

Heaven Sent

Feels Like Heaven

Heaven on Earth

The Best of All

Better for Us

Her Good Thing

Long Time Coming

A Promise of Forever Love

A Love for Tomorrow

Yesterday's Promise

Forgotten

Forgiven

Forsaken

Rain for Christmas (Novella)

Through the Storm

Rain Storm

Latter Rain

Abundant Rain

Former Rain

Anthologies (Editor)

Keeping the Faith

Have A Little Faith

This Far by Faith

EBOOKS

Love Isn't Enough

A Mighty Love

The Blessed One (Blessed and Highly Favored series)

The Wild One (Blessed and Highly Favored Series)

The Preacher's Choice (Blessed and Highly Favored Series)

The Politician's Wife (Blessed and Highly Favored Series)

The Playboy's Redemption (Blessed and Highly Favored Series)

Tears Fall at Night (Praise Him Anyhow Series)

Joy Comes in the Morning (Praise Him Anyhow Series)

A Forever Kind of Love (Praise Him Anyhow Series)

Ramsey's Praise (Praise Him Anyhow Series)

Escape to Love (Praise Him Anyhow Series)

Praise for Christmas (Praise Him Anyhow Series)

His Love Walk (Praise Him Anyhow Series)

Could This Be Love (Praise Him Anyhow Series)

Song of Praise (Praise Him Anyhow Series)

And the Lord shall guide thee continually, and satisfy thy soul in drought, and make fat thy bones: and thou shalt be like a watered garden, and like a spring of water, whose waters fail not." ~ Isaiah 58:11

INTRODUCTION

I have been in a business that I also consider my full-time ministry for 15 years as of this writing. It wasn't easy for me to accept that I had within me a ministry that was also something that required others to pay me for (a business). I always thought that ministry was something you did while volunteering at the church. Later, I came to understand that just as a pastor is very much in ministry while receiving a paycheck for his/her services, so too am I in ministry while receiving payment from the gift God blessed me with.

So, what I want to do in this particular book *Faithful Entrepreneur* is help the person who may be struggling to identify the ministry God has for them. This book is also designed to help you understand the faith needed for the journey. What do I mean by that? Simply this, God's word says, *without faith it is impossible to please Him, because you must first believe that He is and that He is a rewarder of them that diligently seek Him.* So, do you honestly believe that you will have a ministry for God, but you won't have to pray late into night about a bill coming due?What happens when you can't see how any of your vision will come together? Will you trust God for the suddenly? Can you stand in faith believing that God will make sure you have everything needed to get the job done?

Your faith in God is being built from one project to the next. First, God makes a way out of no way for some small something that you need, then you begin to trust Him with an even bigger need... God shows up just in time for that. Now, you're rubbing your hands together for the next project because you know that if God helped you before, there is nothing that will stop Him from helping you again. Plus, your heavenly Father owns the cattle on a thousand hills. He is Alpha and Omega, Beginning and End. There is nothing too hard for the God you serve.

Wasn't He with Daniel in the lions' den? Wasn't He with Shadrach, Meshach and Abednego in the fiery furnace? Listen to me beloved, God has purpose and a calling on your life, all He needs you to do is step out on faith, and He will be there to catch you.

I believe the most important thing we do as Christians, other than living according to the word of God, is to share the love and knowledge of Jesus Christ with a world that is in desperate need of a savior. You might be sitting there reading this book, thinking that the gift you have is insignificant. Trust me I not only understand those feelings, but I had them myself. But let me introduce you to God's principles: One plants, one waters… but God gives the increase.

Your job is to either be planting seed or watering the seed that is already within a person. It is not your concern how, when or what God will then do with that person. Let's say the gift God gave you is that of a seamstress. You start a business and you call it, Anointed Hands Seamstress Shop. One day a customer walks into your shop. She desperately needs alterations for a dress that she plans to wear to a formal event.

While you are working on this lady's dress, she looks at the name of your business and says, "I've never heard anyone call their hands anointed before. Do you really believe that?" As you are stitching this dress, you smile, because you know that God has just given you an opportunity to plant or water a seed in this woman. And so, you share your story with her. The woman pays for her services and then leaves your shop. You don't see this woman again until many years later. You have forgotten about this woman, but she never forgot about you. In fact, the minute she sees you, she runs over to you, excited to tell you how meeting you changed her life. She then tells you that after hearing about how you gave your life to Jesus Christ, she began to hunger and thirst for the same feelings you described, and she is now saved and living for the Lord.

I used the example of a seamstress because I want you to see and understand the gift God gives you doesn't have to be a typical ministry like preaching and teaching in order for you to be a Faithful Entrepreneur.

This book is my love letter to Christian entrepreneurs. It's my pom-poms lifted, cheering you on screaming, "Go get it, cause God said you can have it" plea to all who are called to do something for God. I know that it's not easy to step out on faith and trust that your children won't starve or that you won't lose your home. But if you learn how to make wise decisions coupled with your faith in God, you will get through this entrepreneurial journey.

In this book, we will take on the meaning of faith as it relates to business and ministry. What do I mean by that? Thousands of would-be entrepreneurs give up each year after hitting one road block after the next, but I have learned how to pray for direction and switch gears when need be in order to stay in business. Trust me, if I can do this, you can too. I am no superwoman, just a woman of faith who decided to trust God. So, keep reading and I will show you how faith, prayer and planning will guide your business through tough times and move you towards spiritual and financial success.

I want to show you how your business can also be your ministry. We live in perilous times. Many people have left the church and abandoned their faith in God. Many children now grow up with no sense of who God is or why they would even want to become a Christian. Since we as Christians have the answer they seek, we must explore every opportunity to inform a hurting world about Jesus Christ, the giver of eternal life.

It is given of every man and woman to live and to die. But it is also given of us to dream… to grab hold of God's vision for our lives and run this race until we get to that magnificent finish line. Don't you want to one day hear the Father say, "Well done my good and faithful servant. You have been faithful over a few things, I will make you ruler over many things. Enter now into the joy of the Lord."

In *Faithful Entrepreneur* you will learn how to seek the Lord for your ministry and discover whether or not you can incorporate your ministry in a business that will bring wealth, so you will be able to use the abundance to take care of your family and continue to spread this good news of the Gospel. Planning for success is crucial for an entrepreneur, and I will teach you how to do that as well.

Book 2 of the *Faith and Business Series (Entrepreneur Girl)* deals with starting a business from zero, cash flow, how to go to market with an idea and interviews with other *Faithful Entrepreneurs*. I have also developed *The Faithful Entrepreneur Workbook/Planner*, which will aid you in planning the success of your God-given business.

Beloved, I believe that God wants you to succeed in this life. Doesn't His word tell us that the wealth of the wicked is laid up for the righteous? So, God has put people in place to bless you on this entrepreneurial journey, you just have to learn how to trust God with it all. So, if you're ready for this journey of faith, turn the page and let's get started.

1

THE JOURNEY THAT PROPELLED ME INTO MY MINISTRY

At the age of 26 I felt beaten down and depressed due to living a life of sin. I was tired. One of my closest friends invited me to go to church with her, and at that point I was so miserable that I was willing to do anything to get that feeling off of me, even if it was only for a few hours. But little did I know, God had other plans for me that day.

I thoroughly enjoyed the service, and by the end when Pastor Willie Mitchell made an altar call, I was ready. I remember not only giving my life to God on January 16, 1994, but I also remember getting down on my knees and praying to God. At that moment I had finally found something in my life that brought me an overwhelming feeling of peace, love, and joy. I said to the Lord, "I will serve You, show me how."

I have always been an avid reader, but after giving my life to the Lord, I put away all of the books and only read THE BOOK. For three years straight I read, highlighted, and studied my Bible like it was food to my soul. In some ways the Old Testament replaced the novels I had been reading, because the stories in that part of the Bible read like novels to me. I read my Bible so much that pages would fall out, and I would have to replace my Bible. I read, highlighted, and studied the new Bible until pages fell out of that one as well, and then I would replace another Bible.

God was grooming me for something big, I could feel it. I had no clue what my ministry would be because the only gift I truly knew I had was writing. However, after becoming a Christian, I not only stopped reading novels, I gave up all thought of writing that great American novel; especially since the type of novels I had wanted to write would have been a Jackie Collins knock off. As a teenager, I read *Chances* by the aforementioned author, and I fell in love with a gangster named Gino. From that moment forward, I wanted to write books like that. As a matter of fact, my wanting to write smut-filled books was one of the biggest reasons I didn't become a Christian until I was twenty-six years old.

You see, I knew I had a special gift, but I didn't understand that my gift of writing came from God. So, I sought to pervert the gift by writing all types of nonsense that would not further the cause of

Christ one single bit. But at least I had the good sense to not want to call myself a Christian while promoting something that did not edify the body of Christ. So, I stayed away from church.

When I gave my life to God, I felt a peace that I had never felt in my life. I couldn't believe that I wasted all that time staying away from God while I pursued a career that would not bring me or my readers closer to eternal life in heaven. This should be the eventual goal of every Christian. So, after giving my life to God I declared that I would never read or write novels again, because writing was what kept me from God.

For years, as I read my Bible, I kept praying, asking God to reveal the ministry He had for me. I desperately wanted to please God and do His will with my life. But I had no idea what He wanted from me. I became a greeter, and I thoroughly enjoyed hugging people as they entered the sanctuary for our Wednesday night or Sunday morning services. But I didn't think that was my ministry. I served on the evangelistic team, I served as the head of our singles ministry, director of our drama team, I was the director of our children's Bible study classes, and I served as a mentor for under privileged children. I have also made beds and served food at homeless shelters.

While I enjoyed each ministry that I served in, I never felt as if I had found my calling in life while doing any of them. So, I kept searching, kept praying. Then on an ordinary day, that was just like any other day, except for one simple thing: God was ready to reveal my ministry to me.

A book had been left on my desk at work by a Christian friend of mine. I immediately recognized the book as a novel and was terrified of this thing that sat on my desk. I felt like just opening that book might pull me back into the life of sin I had soundly rejected three years prior.

Just as I was contemplating throwing the novel in the trash and ridding myself of its presence, Scott, the Christian friend I ate lunch with several times a week knocked on my office door. When I turned to greet him, he pointed towards the novel and said, "I left that for you."

Scott was a really nice guy and I knew that he loved the Lord, so I didn't want to be rude, but I had to let him know that I no longer read novels so that he wouldn't leave any more books on my desk. I said, "Thank you, but I don't read novels. I gave that up because I don't like reading that kind of stuff anymore."

To this day, I am so thankful that he didn't just take the book off my desk and go back to his office. Scott shook his head as he told me, "That's Christian fiction. I think you'll like it."

"Christian fiction?" I questioned. I had never heard of such a thing. I thought Christians only read the Bible and self-help books written by preachers.

Thanks to my friend, the first Christian fiction book I ever read was This Present Darkness by Frank Peretti. The novel was about a small town that had been besieged by demons. The devil wanted to conquer the hearts and minds of these people in order to destroy them, but God had other plans. He sent His mighty warrior angels to this town to do battle for the souls of the people.

I was simply blown away by reading this novel. Yes, of course I had already read in the Bible about Gabriel being the messenger angel and Michael the warrior angel. I'd read the Old Testament story when the Prophet Elijah prayed that God would open the eyes of his servant so the man would not be afraid, but rather see all the angels that stood round about them, ready to do battle.

So, I definitely believed in angels. But this was the first fictional book I'd ever read that caused me to feel as if I was right there with the characters and that God was well able to protect ME from any demonic force that tried to come against me or my family. When I was finished reading and closed the book, I sat in my room in total silence for the longest time.

I had given up reading novels and had given up all thought of becoming a writer all because I had fallen in love with Jesus and only wanted to do what was right in His eyes. But after reading this book and seeing the ministry in it, I could no longer deny that writing books could be a ministry, just as preaching, teaching, and evangelizing is a ministry.

It took another seven years before my first book was published, but that was the day that my ministry was formed. And it was formed with a gift that God had put in me from birth. A gift that I had once wanted to pervert with the type of writings I desired to produce. Now, as my eyes were opened, and my desire had changed. I knew without a doubt that it was no mistake that my friend at work laid that book on my desk… it was no mistake that the first Christian fiction book I read had to do with spiritual warfare because most of the books that I now write have a component of spiritual warfare in them. This was the very thing that God wanted to pull out of me from all those years of praying and reading my Bible. I understood and believed in the spiritual battle between heaven and hell, and now God was allowing me to go forth and help to build His kingdom through my writings.

After years of wondering and asking what my ministry was, God didn't just give me a ministry, He also allowed me to utilize my entrepreneurial skills to form a business. I formed my business in 2003. There have been some lean times and some plentifully times during my fifteen years as an entrepreneur, but through it all, I have kept the faith and that's what I want to show you how to do.

2

CAN YOUR MINISTRY ALSO BE YOUR BUSINESS?

As a Christian you should seek God in prayer before beginning any business. If the direction the Lord sends you in clearly shows that your ministry will also be the way you make a living, don't be shy about it. Remember, although we are Christians, we still live on earth and dwell within its economic system; it takes cold hard cash to pay for things like food, shelter, transportation and the like. As the saying goes, closed mouths don't get fed. So, if you spend your days worrying how church folks will receive you once you inform them that the product you have is for sale, then I've got news for you. **You won't be in business long if you give your products away to everyone who wants you to 'bless them' with it**.

God gave you a gift that can feed your family if you will do the work it takes to make it a viable business. But you must first appreciate the simple phrase that the Bible tells us in 1 Timothy 5:18: *"The laborer is worthy of the wages."* Does a farmer spend all year planting and growing a harvest simply to take it to the market and give it away, or does he set a price for his goods?

If you are to be a Faithful Entrepreneur, the first thing you must understand is that it is okay to charge for your services. There will always be people who want something for nothing and accuse you of not being Christian if you don't give them the very thing you earn your living from. But you must not be swayed by that. Now, am I saying that as a Faithful Entrepreneur you can never do a favor or help out someone in need? Not at all. I believe in giving back and you should also. But what I want you to understand is that it is okay to charge for your services because we live in a money economy.

I am dealing with this issue because I know a lot of Christians struggle with the idea of charging for their services or products. I have seen women who could make jewelry, give their product away or barter with another vendor as they swapped products. Please take note of what I am about to say... DON'T DEVALUE YOUR PRODUCTS.

Below is a scenario that I have seen played out too many times...

A businesswoman has items to sell.. Whether it be books, jewelry, apparel, or whatever, she buys her product wholesale, then pays for a vendor table at an event. If the event is out of town, this businesswoman will also have travel expenses (hotel, airfare or rental car, gas, food).

She arrives at the event and sits down behind the vendor table that she paid for. A customer comes to her table. She loves what the businesswoman has to offer and wants the product. But this customer is also a vendor and has a product for sale, so she says to the businesswoman, "Can I trade you, your product for mine?"

In my opinion, the businesswoman who says yes to such a trade makes it seem as if she doesn't value her product, her time, or the money she has already invested in this event. She probably doesn't want the product the other lady is selling and most likely wouldn't have purchased it with her hard-earned money. So, why swap the product that is meant to earn money for the business?

I'm all for supporting other vendors, and if it is a product that I am interested in, I will take my money to that vendor's table and pay for what I want. I would never take one of my books and say, "I really like what you have, can I trade my book for what I want on your table." The problem with doing this, is two-fold. First, you are trading the goods and services that you are supposed to be selling and second, doing such a thing assumes that the other person wants what you have to offer, and they may not want it. But now you've put them in an awkward position, so they begrudgingly accept your product in exchange for theirs.

In truth, I have witnessed this uncomfortable situation on numerous occasions with other vendors. I have even had vendors ask me to barter with them. However, I had no problem with informing them that I have a strict policy not to barter my books. I am at an event to sell the books. And I keep track of my sales for tax purposes.

If you have ever bartered your goods for another person's goods or services, I plead with you now to stop. Doing something like this turns what you do into a hobby rather than a business. Think about it… you can't go into Target and offer them the product you have for one of their products. And why not? Because Target operates as a business and you should too.

Trust in the business/ministry enough to charge a living wage for it. Notice, I said, a living wage, which means I'm not suggesting that you overprice your product just so you can get rich quick. I believe that the people of God should be honest brokers of their products. Yes, you want to turn a profit, so you do not want to low ball yourself. But there is a line between profit and gouging and because you are called by God, I truly believe you'll know when you have crossed that line.

In 3 John 1:2 the Bible says, "Beloved, I wish above all things that thou mayest prosper and be in health, even as thy soul prospereth." So, God wants you to prosper spiritually and financially. He wants you to earn enough money so that you can eat right and treat your body right, so you can be healthy and continue the work that you have been put on this earth to do. Believe in yourself and the worthiness of your calling. Unless you want to get a Go-Fund Me page for your ministry, you will have to charge for the work that God has blessed you to do. And you will have to become comfortable with that fact.

When I first started out, all the money I had was invested in the production of my books. I believed in what I was doing, so I wasn't afraid, but I knew that if I didn't sell books, my daughter and I could be living out of my car because I would lose the house. During this time, one of my cousins told me that he had just PURCHASED a Terri McMillan book and then he asked me to GIVE him my book so he could read it because he loved reading.

He didn't know that those books he wanted me to give him cost me very real money and that I had a lot riding on the success of those books. He just wanted something free and he had a connection to get it. But it kept going through my mind that he PURCHASED the other book that he wanted, so that settled it for me. If people, whether they be friend or family wanted the goods I had for sell, they needed to purchase them, just as they would purchase from others. Because I'm kind hearted, I would certainly give them a discount (smile).

But in the same token, I was never upset with any friend or family member who didn't like to read and therefore wasn't interested in purchasing a book. Don't push your product on people who aren't interested, go out and find customers for your product so you earn a living. If you can't find those paying customers you will be out of business. That is how entrepreneurism works.

I am challenging you to be business minded, but I don't want you to forget the ministry part of your business. Once you are out of the red and your business is no longer do or die, honor opportunities to be a blessing. Prison chaplains contact me on a regular basis because the inmates ask for my books (I'm smiling as I write this because God has allowed me to minister within the prison walls). Whenever I receive the call or an email from a prison chaplain, I mail them out books free of charge. I also donate to book events. But none of this would have been possible if I hadn't decided from the beginning to run my book ministry as a business. If I gave my books away to everyone who asked in the beginning, I wouldn't have lasted this long. Why? Because books are a product, and it cost money to obtain products. If you don't recoup, so you can reorder, you no longer have a business… got it?

Now that we have that settled, let's take on the question, "What's my ministry?" And should I charge for this ministry?" Those are two excellent questions, because I do not believe that every ministry should have a price tag on it. Take what I do… books. The reason there is a price tag on my ministry is because there is a cost to produce the books, there is a cost associated with travel and events. If I don't charge for the books I produce, eventually the money will run out to produce them, and as I stated earlier, I would then be out of business. Also, I am not ashamed that my business makes money that prospers my family because I have bills that must be paid.

When I first gave my life to the Lord and began reading the Bible, I found this scripture in Psalms 37:25 - *I have been young, and now am old; yet have I not seen the righteous forsaken, nor his seed begging bread.* I held onto that scripture with everything I had. I trusted the Lord's word and believed that it was for me too. I grew up poor, lived in the ghetto and fought my way out, but I determined that my seed would never know what it feels like to go hungry or to live in a place where drug addicts roamed the streets day and night, and broke into your house and stole the stuff you worked hard to get.

Because I decided to trust that the scriptures were for me too, God has been faithful. He has used a gift that He gave me to prosper us and my seed hasn't ever had to beg for a thing. My daughter has a good job and she is well able to provide for my grandchildren. And I believe that my grandchildren will become millionaires and if God says so, I will be here to watch it happen. I've already told them I just want a very nice house in my old age... maybe a car or two also. Hey, they'll have all this money simply because I believed God would do it for them, so why not share a little of that wealth with their favorite NaNa?

I don't know what your ministry is or whether it is to be done inside of a church as a volunteer or beyond the walls of the church. You will have to go to God in prayer about that and let Him lead you. But this I do know, if you are reading this book, it is because you want to do a work for God. Maybe you are stuck like I was years ago, not knowing what that work would be. Maybe you know what God has called you to do but are still unsure of how to make it all work. I pray that what I have to say propels you forward in your ministry. Because I truly believe that walking in your rightful ministry brings joy. There's a saying, 'do what you love, and you'll never work a day in your life'. That's how I feel about writing. This isn't work to me, it is my labor of love because I was born to do this. So, now I ask you what is the thing that you would gladly wake up every morning to do even if no one paid you a dime to do it? Or put another way, what are you passionate about?

Many people spend years and years searching for a mysterious calling from God, when He has set it in plain sight. God put it in you to love the very thing that you are called to do. It is that thing you can't stop doing. An artist can't live without paint, a singer seeks out music, an author must write, a preacher will preach to a rock. In the same token, a planner is always finding events to help out with, a person who is detail oriented can't stop organizing things.

Take a moment and look deep within yourself. What is it that you love doing? Don't worry about how you can make a business out of it at this moment. I just want you to describe your passion.

Write it down. I am Passionate about…

_____

_____

_____

_____

_____

_____

_____

_____

3

GOD'S VISION FOR YOUR LIFE

Have you ever attended a vision board party? It's lots of fun to gather with like-minded people to plan and strategize for the next year. The tools normally used in a vision board party include a foam board or sketch pad paper, pencils, markers, magazines, glue, and scissors. The moderator normally instructs the attendees to visualize the life they want to have. They are then encouraged to review magazines and look for pictures of things they want to accomplish or things they want to have in their lives. The attendee then cuts the image out of the magazine and glues it to the foam board.

It is a fun and worthwhile project. But to unlock the type of vision God has for your life it will take more than magazine clippings on a piece of foam board. Unlocking this mystery will prove to be the greatest accomplishment of your life. So, how do you discover God's vision for your life? **Follow the clues**. Be careful though, because so many people miss the clues that are sent by God to show us our destiny. They then either spend a lifetime being unproductive or they go into ministries that God didn't direct them to do in the first place.

Let me ask you a question? How many times have you run across a preacher who obviously didn't belong behind the pulpit? He or she failed to follow the clues for the God-given life he or she was meant to lead. He/She most likely started out in ministry wanting to do something great for God. But God never called this person to preach. He had a whole other ministry designed for this man or woman of God.

Let's say this person was meant to sing. So, every Sunday you find this preacher singing even after the choir has already finished with praise & worship. Now, it's time to preach, but this preacher was meant to be a singer, so he or she simply can't just deliver the message without doing what they were truly born to do. Or let's say he or she is a gifted organizer. So, this pastor spends most of his/her time planning events for the church rather than working on the sermon God needs delivered to His people. But you see, this person was born to organize and plan, so he or she will never be happy leaving the planning to someone else in the church.

I have visited churches like this where the preacher is most definitely an anointed singer whose songs cause you to cry out to God, but his church was very disorganized, and his sermon was disjointed and jumbled.

The thing that then hinders what God is trying to do through us is that we don't think the calling God has for our lives is big enough. Or we allow others to puff us up, to think that God wants more from us, when God never said that. There is nothing wrong with wanting more out of life, but you must possess the skills or talent to handle each level of ministry you aspire to.

Trust me, you don't want to think that you are working to further the kingdom of God when your ministry is actually hindering it because you aren't where God needs you to be. Quick example: After years of trying to figure out what ministry I was supposed to be in, I finally figure it out. I then began writing and traveling the country selling my books. One Sunday I arrive at church and one of the ministers says to me, "God's got an anointing on your life, Sister Vanessa. He's going to do great things with you." I said, "Thank you. I'm am grateful that God has finally shown me what He wants me to do." But then this minister added, "Oh He's not done. You're going to be preaching. Just watch."

The person who said that to me meant well. He truly believed that I had a call on my life, and I do. The only problem was, he wanted more from me than God wanted. I knew even as he said those words that God did not call me to preach. For one, I absolutely hate the idea of having to prepare a sermon every week, my eyes are rolling even as I think about such a thing. And there's one other little problem... I'm a terrible speaker!

Let me clarify that last statement. Because I do accept speaking engagements all the time, but never as a preacher. I would be terrible at that. But I speak to women's ministry groups, singles ministries, book clubs and business events concerning my books and my life story or my entrepreneurial story. Thank God I know whose I am, and what I am and have never allowed people to put me in a place God does not desire for me. Because if God wanted me to do it, He would have given me the ability. Can I get an amen?

So, how do we follow the clues in order to find the ministry God has for each and every one of us? And how do we determine if we can also build a career based on our ministry? These are very good questions because there are people in this world who don't believe that ministers of the Gospel should be paid. I can only assume that they don't think preachers, singers, writers, life coaches and so many other professions live in homes with mortgages. Or maybe they think that God lights up the homes of ministers and keeps those homes warm in the winter and cool in the summer. They also must think that grocery store owners have set aside some fund that will pay for the groceries of every minister who comes looking for food.

Put simply, people who accept the call of God and truly want to minister to God's people in whatever manner God allows are still mandated by the laws of the land to pay their bills. But does that mean I believe all ministry requires payment? No, I do not. I volunteer my services at church all the time. I have served in many church ministries and not once did I ask the church to pay me for my reasonable service to the ministry.

But if God has given you a gift that you desire to use for the furtherance of the gospel, don't let anyone make you feel as if you're doing the wrong thing when you require payment. Because you live on earth, in an economy that requires money for all of your basic needs: food, shelter, clothes, utilities.

Now, let's get to the real issue at hand. How do you know whether God has given you a ministry that is also your business/ career? After giving my life to God in 1994, I remember getting on my knees and praying these words, "I will serve You, Lord. Show me how." From that moment on, I was consumed with the knowledge that I wanted to serve God, I just didn't know how He wanted to use me in ministry; so I kept asking 'What's my ministry?' It took a few years, but the Lord finally made it clear to me that my ministry was writing. What did I do in those years that enabled God to reveal my ministry to me? It is the simple formula I offer to you now: Read. Pray. Seek.

Taking a deeper look at each of these elements will help you discover your destiny/ministry (if you are paying attention to the clues). Let's get started.

READ

By read, I am of course suggesting that you spend time reading the Bible which gives us a vision for how we should live our lives. Within those wondrous pages, you will also read about others who discovered their reason for being (ministry) and how they answered God's call. Let's take Esther for example.

Esther was growing up under the care of her uncle Mordecai. She had no idea that she would become queen of a nation. Nor did she know that her new position (queen) would one day be the very thing that God used to save the Jews. Let's look at chapter 4 in the book of Esther.

Chapter 4

When Mordecai learned [that Haman was conspiring to kill the Jews] he tore his clothes and put on sackcloth and ashes, and went out into the midst of the city. He cried out with a loud and bitter cry. 2 He went as far as the front of the king's gate, for no one *might* enter the king's gate clothed with sackcloth. 3 And in every province where the king's command and decree arrived, *there was* great mourning among the Jews, with fasting, weeping, and wailing; and many lay in sackcloth and ashes.

4 So Esther's maids and eunuchs came and told her, and the queen was deeply distressed. Then she sent garments to clothe Mordecai and take his sackcloth away from him, but he would not accept *them.* 5 Then Esther called Hathach, *one* of the king's eunuchs whom he had appointed to attend her, and she gave him a command concerning Mordecai, to learn what and why this *was.* 6 So Hathach went out to Mordecai in the city square that *was* in front of the king's gate. 7 And Mordecai told him all that had

happened to him, and the sum of money that Haman had promised to pay into the king's treasuries to destroy the Jews. **8** He also gave him a copy of the written decree for their destruction, which was given at Shushan, that he might show it to Esther and explain it to her, and that he might command her to go in to the king to make supplication to him and plead before him for her people. **9** So Hathach returned and told Esther the words of Mordecai.

10 Then Esther spoke to Hathach, and gave him a command for Mordecai: **11** "All the king's servants and the people of the king's provinces know that any man or woman who goes into the inner court to the king, who has not been called, *he has* but one law: put *all* to death, except the one to whom the king holds out the golden scepter, that he may live. Yet I myself have not been called to go in to the king these thirty days." **12** So they told Mordecai Esther's words.

13 And Mordecai told *them* to answer Esther: "Do not think in your heart that you will escape in the king's palace any more than all the other Jews. **14** For if you remain completely silent at this time, relief and deliverance will arise for the Jews from another place, but you and your father's house will perish. Yet who knows whether you have come to the kingdom for *such* a time as this?"

15 Then Esther told *them* to reply to Mordecai: **16** "Go, gather all the Jews who are present in Shushan, and fast for me; neither eat nor drink for three days, night or day. My maids and I will fast likewise. And so I will go to the king, which *is* against the law; and if I perish, I perish!"

You may want to read the entire story of Esther, or at least chapters 4 thru 8. In those chapters you will read how Esther discovered who she was and what she was called to do that would save the lives of her people.

Esther's ministry was to her husband the king. Because she had spent years being good to her king/husband, when the time came to request something of him that would not only save her life, but the lives of the Jewish people, the king immediately acted upon her request. After reading this story, I realized that each of us have a calling in life. God may not have revealed it to us as of yet, but He is setting everything up for us to be in position to do what He has called us to do. Our job is to respond to the call when we hear it.

Many people think that going to church and paying tithes is all that is required of Christians. But I say, that person missed the entire meaning of the Parable of the Talents. You see, I believe that God has put certain talents and/or gifts in each us. It is our job to find our gift or talent and use it to advance the kingdom of God. If you don't believe me. Let's read the Parable of the Talents in Matthew 25: 14-29.

Matthew 25: 14-29

14 "For *the kingdom of heaven is* like a man traveling to a far country, *who* called his own servants and delivered his goods to them. **15** And to one he gave five talents, to another two, and to another one, to each according to his own ability; and immediately he went on a journey. **16** Then he who had received the five talents went and traded with them, and made another five talents. **17** And likewise he who *had received* two gained two more also. **18** But he who had received one went and dug in the ground, and hid his lord's money. **19** After a long time the lord of those servants came and settled accounts with them.

20 "So he who had received five talents came and brought five other talents, saying, 'Lord, you delivered to me five talents; look, I have gained five more talents besides them.' **21** His lord said to him, 'Well *done,* good and faithful servant; you were faithful over a few things, I will make you ruler over many things. Enter into the joy of your lord.' **22** He also who had received two talents came and said, 'Lord, you delivered to me two talents; look, I have gained two more talents besides them.' **23** His lord said to him, 'Well *done,* good and faithful servant; you have been faithful over a few things, I will make you ruler over many things. Enter into the joy of your lord.'

24 "Then he who had received the one talent came and said, 'Lord, I knew you to be a hard man, reaping where you have not sown, and gathering where you have not scattered seed. **25** And I was afraid, and went and hid your talent in the ground. Look, *there* you have *what is* yours.'

26 "But his lord answered and said to him, 'You wicked and lazy servant, you knew that I reap where I have not sown, and gather where I have not scattered seed. **27** So you ought to have deposited my money with the bankers, and at my coming I would have received back my own with interest. **28** Therefore take the talent from him, and give *it* to him who has ten talents.

29 'For to everyone who has, more will be given, and he will have abundance; but from him who does not have, even what he has will be taken away.

As I have told many people, I have one gift (talent). Writing is my gift. And there was a point in my life when I decided that I would never write again… I would take my one talent and bury it and present it back to God, unused and unharmed by this cruel, cruel world. But reading the Parable of the Talents helped me to understand that if God gives us something, He wants us to be fruitful with it.

Are you beginning to see how reading the scriptures can strengthen and build your faith to help you not only discover your ministry, but to act on it and make it do what God wants it to do?

In your Bible reading time, search out the scriptures for stories, parables or situations that build your faith and encourage you concerning the ministry/business God has given you.

Scripture: _____

What is God saying to you:

_____

_____

_____

_____

_____

Scripture: _____

What is God saying to you:

_____

_____

_____

_____

_____

Scripture: _____

What is God saying to you:

_____

_____

_____

_____

_____

PRAY

How many times have you heard, _Prayer Changes Things_? Do you believe it? I believed it from the moment I gave my life to God because it was prayer that brought me to the altar in the first place.

I gave my life to God the winter of 1994. But let me explain how a person who had given up on God, even happened to be in church that day. I had always believed in God and knew that I was supposed to serve Him in some manner. I've already discussed how I discovered that writing was my ministry, but before I could discover that, I had to first accept Jesus as my Lord and savior.

Back then, I was bitter for so many reasons. One of my closest friends had died of heart problems at the age of 26. I had been in one bad relationship after the next and I was raising a child on my own and was barely able to make ends meet. So, God wasn't on my radar. But there was an older woman on my job whom I had become friends with. She and I would eat lunch together every day. I would tell her about all my problems and about all the night clubs I went to and the men I dated at the time.

Her name was Louise Jordan, and I am thankful to this day that I befriended her because she was a praying woman. Louise went to church every morning at 6am and prayed before she came to work. I didn't know it at the time, but Louise was calling my name out to God every morning, asking Him to stop me from going out to night clubs, because she was so afraid that something terrible would happen to me if I kept hanging out with the kind of people I had been hanging out with.

Can you guess what happened next? Let me tell you... One Friday, Louise and I were leaving work. As we stood at the elevator waiting for it to open, she asked, "Are you going to Majestic tonight?" The reason she asked about that particular club was because I went to a different club depending on the day of the week. I was addicted to the night life and went out on Monday, Wednesday, Friday, and Saturday. On each of those nights I made my way to the hotspot for that night, and on Fridays it was Majestic.

But on that day, I took a moment to think about Louise's question and then I turned to her and said, "No, I'm not going out tonight." I remember taking a deep breath and sighing as if I was so very tired and then I add, "As a matter a fact, I don't think I'm going out ever again." And from that day until this very day, I have not stepped one foot inside of a night club. How else can you explain something like that except that God answered Louise's prayer for me.

That incident happened in September of 1993. Louise could have shouted the victory, stopped going to early morning prayer after I stopped going out to night clubs because she had received what she asked God for. But her assignment wasn't finished yet. Instead of getting extra sleep in the morning, she continued to go to early morning prayer from September to January, but now she was asking God to save my soul.

Louise didn't tell me about her prayers until she had received the full manifestation of them. On January 16, 1994, I finally could take no more. God had been pulling on me so strong. My sister had even given me a Bible for Christmas in 1993. I scoffed at her gift and laughed with my friends about it. But it was not long after receiving that gift that I experienced a nightmare in which I thought I was in hell.

You see, I had been telling people for about a year or so, that I didn't care anymore. You got treated bad on earth, so if I went to hell and they treated me bad it would be just another day as far as I was concerned. Thanks be to God that He heard my foolish talk and decided to show me how much worse hell is than anything I had imagined. A week after God allowed me to have that nightmare, I went to church and gave my life to Him and haven't looked back since. Louise was then able to get a little more sleep in the mornings if she wanted, because she was no longer mandated to get up early and pray for me.

After I gave my life to God, Louise told me all that she had been doing. This was my first encounter with the power of prayer. Through the years, I have seen how God has turned situations around for people that I have prayed for and even situations in my own life. So I'm a believer.

I remember praying about my ministry when I first became a Christian. I could feel down deep in my soul that God wanted me to do something, but I honestly didn't know what. When I gave my life to God, I decided right then and there that I would never write again. Wanting to be a writer was the thing that had kept me from accepting the Lord Jesus Christ into my life, but once I finally gave my life to

God, I realized that falling in love with Jesus was the best thing I'd ever done. I then felt as if I had wasted my life chasing this dream of being a writer when I could have been serving God. So, I put down my pen and paper (in the 90s, if you were writing, it was on a typewriter or pen and note pad). But I still kept praying and believing that God would one day reveal my ministry to me.

How do we pray to God when seeking our ministry? Your prayer doesn't have to be anything elaborate. Fire doesn't have to come down from heaven for you to believe that God heard your prayer. Just go to the Father and say, as I did many, many years ago, "Lord, I will serve You. Show me how."

It was as simple as that. I wanted to serve God, so I asked Him to show me how. I didn't pray about it every day. But whenever I thought about how I could be used by God, I would talk to the Lord about how I was feeling and ask Him once again to show me my ministry. I had a full-time job which eventually became my career through one promotion after another. So, I never imagined that the ministry God had for me would cause me to step out on faith and pursue it as my full-time occupation.

But prayer not only changes things… it moves God into action on your behalf. You must be paying attention, though. Because you can easily miss the answer to your prayers if you're not careful.

SEEK

This generation doesn't know what it's like to be lost while trying to find a certain location. In the world we now live in, all you have to do is turn on your GPS and the system searches for the location and then gives you the step-by-step directions to your destination.

Understanding the concept of the GPS will help you understand the concept of seeking God for your ministry and then accepting His directions as He leads you to your appointed destination.

Let me detail how seeking God concerning my ministry led straight to the gift God had for me: As I previously stated, I knew that I could write and that I desired to write. But for reasons already mentioned, I figured that writing was not what God had for me. I put it out of my mind and I was prepared to live without the very thing that had been such a part of me for as long as I could remember.

As I attended church, read my Bible, and volunteering in numerous capacities, I kept asking God what He wanted me to do. I wasn't overly anxious about it, because I was laboring in the ministry. I was a greeter, I worked on the evangelist team, director of the drama team, singles ministry and director of the children's Bible study classes. I was ordained as a minister by my former church, and I was happy. But in each and every ministry that I served in I would ask God, "Is this it? Is this what You want from me? If the answer was yes, I would have continued serving God in whatever manner He saw fit.

Then one day, a few years after the first time I prayed and asked God to show me how to serve Him, something happened that changed everything. Remember the novel my co-worker left on my desk? Anyone who knows what I do now, understands how God put that single action in place to move me toward my destiny.

For two to three years all I did was read my Bible. I read my Bible so much that pages started falling out. And even that was a part of God's plan, because God knew I would need to understand the scriptures in order to write the kind of Christian fiction He desired for me to write.

Reading This Present Darkness by Frank Peritti took blinders off my eyes. I was mesmerized from beginning to end. The book had main characters and love interests just as the countless other novels I had read. But this one was like nothing I had ever read because it also had angels battling demons on behalf of God's people. This was the first time I had read a novel where I felt the power of God come alive in the midst of the story. From that moment on, I knew what God had predestined me to do from birth… my ministry was writing. And I would soon become (not the first) but one of the first African American Christian fiction authors.

My first Christian fiction title (Former Rain) released in May 2003, however, if you will allow me a moment to get technical; I began writing that book in 1996. So, if I hadn't been such a procrastinator, I could have been the first. I only mention that to encourage you not to lose focus. If God has given you a ministry, then you must act on it. Get up and do what you were born to do!

Basically, I discovered that the thing I was called to do was the very thing I had fallen in love with from a young age. At the age of eight, my father told me a story about a rat, but I didn't know it was a rat at first. The way he described the thing, I just knew it was something beautiful and awesome. When I found out the story was about a rat, I immediately wanted to do what he had just done right before my eyes… turn something hideous into beauty and majesty.

I began telling people that I was going to be a writer. I had no idea how to make that happen, I just knew that the writing bug was in me and it had to come out. In high school, I wrote and sold poems. I then began writing stage plays. At the age of twenty-four, my first play was performed to a live audience. I loved writing, but it had been the very thing that I was willing to give up, in order to serve.

I truly believe that once God saw that I loved Him more than the gift that He had given me, He then knew that he could reveal my assignment to me and that I wouldn't try to pervert the assignment, as I had once wanted to do. My assignment had been formed in me at the age of eight. Remember how I told you after listening to my father's story I wanted to turn the hideous into beauty and majesty? Well, I now write about characters who are hideous when you first meet them. They are consumed by sin, until Jesus steps in and turns their lives around, then they become beautiful in the sight of God. So, even that story my father told me as a young child was a clue God was sending to me.

My name means butterfly. Think about the butterfly for a moment. It does not start off beautiful and full of colors. It begins its life as a caterpillar. And even though we smile when watching a butterfly flutter those beautiful wings as it flies, we have very different feeling when seeing a hideous caterpillar. So, even the name given to me at birth was no mistake. Once I had followed the clues, God wanted me to see that He had this ministry in mind for me from birth.

Ask yourself, "What is it that God has for me to do?" Have you noticed any clues that God has inserted into your life to direct you to your destiny? As I followed the clues, I discovered that I wasn't just supposed to write, but I was supposed to write about caterpillars being turned into butterflies by the power of my Lord and Savior, Jesus Christ. See how specific the clues in my life were? Are you paying attention or living your life clueless? If your GPS is taking you off course, recharge it with the Word of God and prayer.

If you know what you've been put on this earth to do, but still haven't found a way to get to it, ask yourself this: Is your assignment being delayed because God needs to work on your heart? Does He need to get you to the point that you would lay down the gift, for the Giver?

If this is you, and you have denied God because the agenda that you have for your life doesn't include Him. You know that God is calling you to develop a closer relationship with Him. But you say to yourself, 'If I move closer to God, then I have to give up this or that'. Let me suggest that you give whatever it is up, and allow God to give it back to you, if that is the thing He wants for your life.

I can't promise you that pursuing God's chosen ministry for your life will make you a multi-millionaire, or that you'll become famous. But what I can promise you is that if you find YOUR reason for being... the thing that God predestined YOU to do, you will one day hear the words, 'Well done, my good and faithful servant,' and God will supply all your needs according to His riches in glory. My Lord gives the best insurance plans and retirement plans. I'm a living witness that He can take you places far beyond your imagination.

If you still don't know what your ministry is, keep seeking it out. Dig deep within. Ask yourself, what do I love doing? What would I do for free? Answering those questions will help you discover your passion. Once you know what you are passionate about, ask yourself how you can use that passion for God?

As you continue to seek, God will reveal the plan to you in due time. If the ministry God has given you is also a business from which you will earn money, don't shy away from it. Remember, a pastor is called to preach by God, but that doesn't stop him or her from collecting their paycheck. So, it shouldn't stop you either.

Examples of gifts from God that people have turned into a business

We readily understand that a singer can use his or her gift to sing gospel music. A preacher uses his or her gift to minister to God's people. A writer can use his or her gift to minister through the written word. But let's say God has gifted you with organizational skills. Many people with this gift have become Virtual Assistants. How can a Virtual Assistant use her gift to further God's kingdom? Simple, link up with a ministry and use the organizational skills to move that ministry to the next level. It may not be a ministry that God is directing you to as a virtual assistant. We don't know the plans of God. But you have to trust Him wherever He leads you. There may be someone in an organization that God needs you to minister His Word or the love of God to. Do His will and let Him lead you.

Have you ever heard of the Ministry of Helps? This spiritual gift is found in 1 Corinthians 12:28: *"And God hath set some in the church, first apostles, secondarily prophets, thirdly teachers, after that miracles, then gifts of healings, helps, governments, diversities of tongues."*

The exact meaning of the gift of helps is somewhat obscure, but "helps" translated means literally, "to relieve, succor, participate in, and/or support." Those with the gift of helps are those who can provide assistance to others in the church, hopefully, with compassion and grace. This can be done in numerous ways, from helping individuals with daily assignments to assisting in the administration of the affairs of the church.

People with the gift of helps can use this gift in their own enterprises as well as in the church. I just heard a woman discussing her business on the radio the other day. What does she do? She has a business model that coaches mothers on ways to start and grow a home-based business so they can raise their own children rather than drop them off at daycare centers. I know a lot of women who would love to have a business that allows them to stay home with their kids.

So, this woman is using her God-given gift of "helps" to assist mothers. Think about how much more piece of mind that mother will have if she is able to earn a living and stay at home and raise her children. Now you tell me God isn't interested in a ministry like that. Don't you think a woman with a ministry like that should earn money from her gift so that she can pay her bills and be able to continue helping mothers?

Many people with the gift of helps also perform well as party planners or life coaches. Can you think of other businesses a woman with the gift of helps could thrive in?

Name three businesses for someone with the gift of helps.

1 _____

2 _____

3 _____

If you have the gift of helps, can you name (1) business that you would thrive in? Why?

_____

_____

_____

_____

_____

_____

4

FAITH YOUR WAY THROUGH IT

Many people let finances stop them from starting the ministry/ business God is directing them to start. But I am here to tell you that if God has called you to it, then He will provide the finances. All you need is enough faith to believe that God will never leave you, nor forsake you. Let me give you a few examples from my own business life.

Although I have had (4) different publishers within the 15 years I have been a published author, it didn't start out like that. When I finished my first Christian fiction title *Former Rain* I didn't shop the book around. I was so excited to have finally finished a book that I wanted to get it out to the public as soon as possible. So, I self-published my first book.

Ebooks were not a thing back in 2003. So, to self-publish, I needed to get several thousands of copies of my book so that I could get out there and sell it. But here's the thing, I didn't have any money to do this. I was a single mother at the time, who had purchased a home just three before beginning my writing career. So, although my career in Corporate America was going well and I was earning good money… I had bills that had to be paid on the regular.

But none of those reasons stopped me. Once I had finally finished my first book, I believed without a shadow of a doubt that this is what God had for me. And if He had this ministry in mind for me, then He would make a way. So, I prayed, asking God for the provisions and then I got to work.

I took pre-orders for a book that I had not published yet, and about a hundred people purchased the book. I couldn't believe it, but they actually purchased the book that wasn't a book yet. My friends and I then put on a fish fry and even a yard sale. Whatever it took, we did it. I earned enough money to pay for my first 3,000 copies of Former Rain; now all I had to do was find someplace to sell these books.

Three thousand books may sound like a lot for someone self-publishing, with no former publishing experience and certainly no platform or speaking circuit. But let me brag on my God for a minute, because I not only sold those copies in bookstores, military bases, book conferences, and from the trunk of my car… but that book has seen four reprints from my original company (Butterfly Press). Then I sold the book to a publisher who in turn had to reprint it numerous times themselves.

To this day, Former Rain is still my most beloved book by my readers. But it never would have seen the light of day if I hadn't trusted God enough to take action. You see, the reason many people allow their dreams to be buried with them is because they think after praying for God to help them, all they have to do is continue to sit there and wait on some miraculous sign to show them the way has been cleared for them. But my Bible tells me that God has given me everything I need to succeed.

Ephesians 3:20-21

20 Now to Him who is able to do exceedingly abundantly above all that we ask or think, according to the power that works in us, **21** to Him *be* glory in the church by Christ Jesus to all generations, forever and ever. Amen.

The key words in those scriptures are 'according to the power that works in us' or shall I say, 'the power that works in YOU.' Because by gifting you with whatever ability God has gifted you with, He gave you the power to go out into this world and make your way. Too many people sit around waiting on God, but the truth is God is waiting on you to accept your rightful place. There is a gift inside of you that the world needs. The gift God has given you may change someone's perspective and cause them to give their life to Christ. In my opinion, that is reason enough to get up every morning and work like nothing else matters.

You may be saying to yourself, okay, I get that God has given me a gift and that I am supposed to do something with it, but there are so many obstacles. And I would agree with you. There are always going to be obstacles standing in your way... this is not easy. But those obstacles come to challenge your faith.

I'm not asking you to ignore the obstacles or act as if they don't exist. But what I am saying is, see the obstacle and then give it to God as you step out on faith anyway. Let me give you a few more examples of how this principle has helped me in my business life.

I know there are a lot of believers out there who think you need years of planning and an entire committee of folks in agreement with your vision before it can come to pass... but I say, where's the faith in that? I already told you how I began my self-publishing career with a prayer, a dream and no money... but God! Now I'd like to break down other adventures in my business that I had to faith my way through.

The year was 2005. I now had three books published (Former Rain, Abundant Rain & Latter Rain). I had formed a business and had two partners working with me. It was at that time that I decided I wanted to do another stage play. The stage play would be based on my second book, Abundant Rain. We were making good money from the book sales because I was traveling all over the country doing signings.

The money that funded my travels became a hinderance for the stage play I wanted to do, because we just didn't have the extra money because I was using it for travel expenses. But if I didn't travel to sell the books, the money would stop rolling in (ebooks were not a factor at that time). The two obstacles in the way of making my stage play were lack of finances and time. I needed to find the time to put a cast of characters together and direct them. But the way I was earning money was based on my travels and my book sales.

2005 was also the year that I trusted God enough to step away from my career in Corporate America and become a full-time writer. Even though no other finances would be coming in from anywhere else if I didn't go out and bring them in, this was something I wanted to do, and I was willing to risk it, because I know one thing for sure… God is on my side.

So, we rented meeting rooms for the casting calls, found the actors, had them sign contracts which guaranteed that they would be paid. I had no idea where we would stage the play, but I knew that I couldn't afford places that required payments for everyone from stage hands to security. But God came through for me in that as well. It just so happened that the VA (Veterans Administration) had a building that we could use for the performance, complete with a stage and comfortable seating for the audience. The price the VA asked for was $500, and I gladly paid it because I knew that other places would have charged thousands of dollars for what I wanted to do. Full disclosure, I was back on the road selling books in order to cover the bills associated with that production, but God got me through it. I'm still happy to have done that production and look forward to doing many more in the coming years.

In 2016, I could no longer travel due to a car accident that left me with a broken ankle and panic attacks when I attempted to drive on the highway. I discuss more about this in the chapter, Faith for the Lean Times. Bottom line is, I had to find another way to reach out to my readers since I couldn't go to them. After praying about the situation, my daughter came into my room one day and said, "Why don't you do a retreat for readers." My first thought was planning a retreat would be too hard… too expensive. But as I kept thinking about it, I began to ask, why not? Why couldn't I do this?

After praying about the situation, I came up with a name for my retreat (Christian Book Lover's Retreat). My daughter thought that I shouldn't make the event about Christian books and readers who love Christian books, she thought more people would come if I opened it to all genres. But I told her that serving God is all I know. So, if I do a retreat, it will be about the God that I know. I had to hold on to my faith and believe that the people would show up even though I wasn't offering an event that was full of booty shaking and erotic parties.

There was a brand-new Embassy Suites down the street from where I live. The lobby was gorgeous, and the hotel rooms were plush, and my guests would receive a free breakfast; who could ask for more? Now all I had to do was convince the manager to allow me to use the place even though I didn't have the money to pay for any of the meeting rooms or hotel rooms that I requested. Nor had I signed anyone up for this retreat yet.

What does the Bible tell us in Hebrews 11:1:"*Now faith is the substance of things hoped for, the evidence of things not seen.*" So, in order to step out in faith, I had to first believe that my God was well able to make this happen for me. Not only did that manager write up a contract for those rooms, she did it without receiving any money from me. I was honest with her and informed her that I would be able to pay once I received registrations in from all the people who would be attending my retreat. She gave me a few weeks to make an initial payment and then I went to work on this new venture.

I laugh about that now, because if no one showed up to my first retreat, I would have been on the hook to that hotel for about $80,000, ouch! But what did I tell you before? My God is able to make all grace abound towards me, according to the power that works in us (ME) or (YOU).

Once I had the location secured, I began seriously talking to my readers and author friends about the Christian Book Lover's Retreat. One of the authors, Rhonda McKnight, knew how to design websites, so she did the CBLR website for FREE. Once we had the website up and running, I started promoting the event to the Christian authors and book readers.

Most people would have waited until they had every t crossed and every i dotted. But in truth, I don't work like that. I have faith'd my way through all of my business ventures, and God has always come through for me. As a matter of fact, while planning the retreat, I discovered that I already knew the people I needed to accomplish my goal. Jacquelin Thomas, another Christian fiction author, had worked as an event planner and was able to provide me with a spreadsheet that helped me track spending and ensure that I could budget everything in order to spend wisely. Pat Simmons, another author friend of mine had been working as a publicist for another book conference for years, and she was more than willing to come on board and help us promote the CBLR. The Christian Book Lover's Retreat is now an annual event that grows bigger each and every year… all glory to God!

God is good, and He will not leave us stranded in the midst of doing a good work for the kingdom. But you have to be very sure that the work you're doing is for the kingdom of God and not just to enrich yourself if you are expecting God to show up and show out on your behalf.

Sometimes your belief in God is all you have. But believe me, if God has given you a gift, He wants you to find a way to use that gift to glorify Him. So, I'm telling you what I know, faith in God is all you need to begin the work. Then with planning, and trusting that God will provide the provision, the work gets done. My first pastor, Pastor Willie Mitchell used to say, Faith + Patience = The Promise. When it comes to business, I have learned that:

Faith + A Plan = Success

Even though I faith my way through a lot of my business ideas, I do stop along the way to etch out a plan for success. We will discuss more of that in the next chapter.

5

HOW TO PLAN FOR SUCCESS

You've heard it said numerous times, "If you fail to plan, you plan to fail," but many in Christiandom think that all we have to do is pray and then God rains everything we need down from heaven just as He did with the manna that was provided to the Israelites. They use scriptures like: "Many are the plans in a man's heart, but it is the Lord's purpose that prevails." ~ Proverbs 19:21

Or

"Unless the Lord build the house, they labor in vain who build it;" ~ Psalm 127:1

Some have used these scriptures to justify why they don't have to do anything in order to see their dreams manifest. Now, I'm not saying that God needs our help to get anything done, but why did He create us if we're not supposed to do anything? People who just sit back and wait for life to happen to them totally discount the scriptures that discuss planning, such as 1 Kings 6:38:

"And in the eleventh year, in the month of Bul, which is the eighth month, the house was finished in all its details and according to all its plans. So he was seven years in building it."

Or 1 Chronicles 28:11:

"Then David gave his son Solomon the plans for the vestibule, its houses, its treasuries, its upper chambers, its inner chambers, and the place of the mercy seat;"

These scriptures clearly show that the workers on the project took time to plan it out. I don't want to spend months writing a book with no idea of how I'm going to sell it once I'm finished. So, the writing is one part of the work that I do, but the plan for sales is another part. Your goal in any area of business/ministry is to figure out how you'll go to market with this great idea or product that you have. Even though our faith is in God, we cannot just sit back and hope things turn out the way we want them to.

Let's look at Proverbs 10:4-5: *"He becometh poor that dealeth with a slack hand: but the hand of the diligent maketh rich. He that gathereth in summer is a wise son: but he that sleepeth in harvest is a son that causeth shame."*

What is God telling us in these scriptures? I truly believe that God wants the best for His people, and He is showing us the way to get everything that He has for us... we must get up every morning and (gather) work toward our dreams and goals. We can't ask God why He didn't help us if we aren't doing our part. Because as the above scriptures says, "He becometh poor that dealeth with a slack hand". Translation, doing nothing, brings nothing.

I recently met a woman who told me that from the time she was a little girl, she had visions and dreams where she traveled the world with a briefcase in her hand. Low and behold as she grew up, this woman became a missionary, traveling all over the world for the Lord's glory. Later in life, she became a full-fledged businesswoman with briefcase in hand. So, those were two separate missions from God. But if she had not been following the clues, and God's direction, she could have easily thought that she was supposed to be a businesswoman at the time she was traveling. But that was not God's vision for her life. And if she had not made plans for each separate part of her ministry, neither of them would have taken place. She would still be at home dreaming.

Let's take my writing career for example. While writing my first book, I didn't just sit around dreaming of all the success I would have as an author. I researched and developed my business plan. The idea of a writing business plan sounds scary to some, but it will help you lock down what your business is, how it will function, and how you will make money doing it. You can find tons of business plan templates online, but let's walk through what a business plan looks like. There will be at least (6) sections to your business plan. Depending on the type of business, you may need more sections or fewer; as you research you will be the judge of whether your plan needs more information or less.

Section 1: Executive Summary

In an executive summary you will first create your mission statement (if you desire) then describe your business. What does your business look like? Who are the owners and the management team? Do you have an advisory board? What is the main product(s) that will be sold in your business? In a paragraph, describe your target audience (your customer base). Then describe what unique, improved or cost consequence service you will offer that will sway this audience to what you have to offer.

Note: Please understand the entire world is not your customer base. When you begin a business, it is wise to narrow your base down so that you can focus your products on a particular group.

Section 2: Business/Industry Overview

In this section, you will provide an overview of the industry and then provide information on how your business will compete in this industry. This is where research is needed. Read articles and books on businesses that are similar to yours, study market trends, etc.

Section 3: Market Analysis and the Competition

In this section, you will further define the target market for your product or service. Describe the need for your product or service. Review existing competitor sales and then estimate what your sales would be based on their sales (research-Google is a good place to start. There are also tons of business books on the subject).

Here is an example:

	Competitor #1	Competitor #2	Your Business
Industry Estimate			
Annual Income	$3,000,000	$1,000,000	$
# of Employees	10	5	_____
Cost of Product	Low cost	High cost	_____
Quality	Good	Very Good	_____

Section 4: Sales and Marketing Plan

This is where you will describe how you intend to entice customers to buy your product or services. A lot of thought should go into this section. So, I will take time to describe each area of your sales and marketing section.

*Product or Service - even though you've already described your product or service in the business overview section, add that description as a reminder of what your business is about while you plan your sales and marketing strategy.

*Pricing Strategy - take a moment to figure out how much your product costs to make. Will you have to travel to sell it? How much will your travel cost be? What is your break-even point on this product? How much can you sell it for to make a profit? Will your price be the same as your competitors, higher or lower? Will you start off with a sale to increase the interest in your product? After reviewing those items, then you can decide the price point you will go to market with.

*Sales and Distribution - How will you get your product to market? Will you use a distributor? Will you sell wholesale, retail or both? What type of packaging will be required? How will you ship the product, and how will you receive payment?

*Advertising and Promotion - Will you pay for advertising? What media will you use to get the word out that your product is available? Will you do Facebook ads or ads on Twitter? Will you go door to door? What marketing material will you use... postcards, business cards, flyers, brochures, bookmarks?

Section 5 - Operating Plan

In this section, you will outline the physical needs of the business such as: where will the office be (home office or rental space); will you need a warehouse to store product or retail space; what equipment, inventory and supplies or staff will you need to make this business functional? Certain businesses will need a very detailed operating plan (especially if you are seeking funding for the business). Take a few moments to review the questions I posed for the operating plan and ask yourself which of these areas will be needed for your business. Then write out your wish list for how you want your business to operate.

Section 6 - Financial Plan

If you need financing or want to attract investors, then you'll want to make this section shine. It needs to indicate that your business has the potential to grow. All of the items you'll address in your financial plan section can be done on excel spreadsheets. You will need a separate excel sheet for each item we are about to discuss:

*Income Statement - This is where you will list items like revenue, expenses, and profit. If you are a start-up business, you'll want to do monthly income statements. Once you have a full year under your belt, then do yearly income statements. I am providing an example of an income statement, so you'll understand how you should do one and the items you'll need to keep track of. See below:

Sample Consulting Company

Income Statement

For the Year Ending December 31, 2017

Revenue:

 Consulting revenue earned $92,500

Expenses

Salaries	$42,500	
Supplies	1,950	
Rent	6,000	
Insurance	950	
Advertising	250	
Equipment depreciation	900	
Interest on loan	450	$53,000
Income before income tax		$29,500
Income tax expense		11,500
Net income		$18,000

When I began my business, I had to find unconventional ways of raising money because no one was going to loan me any money when I had no viable proof that my business could make money. Once I was in business a few years and could show income statements, I was then able to get the funding I needed for special projects. So, do those income statements and file your taxes; they will pay off for you down the road.

*Cash Flow Projections - A cash flow projection shows the amount of money you anticipate earning and the expenses associated with those earnings. This form shows how you manage your cash flow and helps lenders know whether you are a good credit risk.

*Balance sheet - This spreadsheet is a snapshot summary of the assets, liabilities, and equity of your business. In my opinion, this particular spreadsheet is the most time consuming and might be the most useless. I have never been asked for my balance sheet. So, if you want to skip this step, you probably could without any problems. However, if it is needed for your business, you can google a few examples and be able to complete it.

Now take a deep breath, because once you have completed those steps you will have a serious plan to move your business forward. But what if you just can't wrap your mind around doing a full-fledged business plan because you are at the beginning stages of your business and you just don't have all the answers yet? Then might I suggest an abbreviated form of a business plan.

You will have to determine for yourself which part of a business plan is most important to getting you to your end result, and then put a laser focus on that part of your plan. For me it was marketing. Since no one was offering to loan me any money for my business venture when I began my business, I had to be very strategic in how and where I spent money. So, here are a few things I pulled out of my marketing strategy and focused on.

Step 1 - Tell people about the book

Step 2 - Find places to sell the book

Step 3 - Find ways to reach readers

*Step 1 - Tell People About the Book

In 2003 when my first book released, there was no such thing as Facebook or Twitter. So, I had to be intentional about the way I would let people know about my books. One of the things I did was to order about 5,000 postcards. I mailed the postcards to people, and I handed them out to everyone I came in contact with. I developed an email list and would send out emails to readers whenever I had a new book or a book signing. I asked friends to tell their friends about my books.

When social media avenues came into play, I incorporated those into my 'tell people about the book' strategy. I am intentional about the people I ask to friend on Facebook, Twitter, or Instagram. I am looking for readers who enjoy Christian fiction, so I wouldn't ask someone who only reads erotica or spy thrillers to join my page. I don't have anything against those people, but I know that someone who does not read Christian fiction would not be interested in the product that I have to sell.

I also don't invite Christians who don't like to read to join my page. I certainly have nothing against Christians, since I am one myself, but the primary reason I am on social media is to promote my products, so I focus on people who are interested in the products I have to promote, and that is my suggestion to you as well.

Too many people spin their wheels trying to promote their products to friends and family who aren't interested in what you have to sell. Then the seller becomes angry because in their mind no one wants to support their vision. When the reality is, they have focused too much energy on people who aren't their target market and not enough energy on their target market.

When you are telling people about your product, most of the people you run into will not be your target market. That's okay, as long as you know how to keep it moving. Don't badger anyone about buying a product they clearly don't want. If you believe in yourself and in your product, you'll quickly realize, as the saying goes, 'one monkey don't stop no show.' Put another way, just because one person is not interested doesn't mean that your product is doomed for failure. Find your target audience and promote your product to those people.

*Step 2 - Find a place to sell my book

After I told everyone I could think of about my book and sold as many copies from word of mouth as I could, I then had to plan out what I would do next. You see, I ordered 3,000 copies of my first book (Former Rain) so I couldn't just sit in the house re-reading that book and patting myself on the back for how beautifully the words flowed... believe it or not, I knew someone who did that. She told me that she often re-read that one book that she wrote as she sat in her house waiting for someone to call and ask her to attend an event to speak about this book.

It has been 15 years since my first book released and I had that conversation with the other author. As of this writing, have 26 novels and 16 novellas written, while she has completely left the writing business and still only has that one book. Why do I tell you this, because life takes action. You cannot sit in the dreamer's seat when it is time to work.

*Step 3 - Find ways to reach readers

One of the things that I think was important to the growth of my business was doing a mailing list. Every event that I signed books at, I would have my mailing list on the table. When someone purchased a book, I would ask them to sign my mailing list because I wanted to be able to contact those readers when my next book released.

So, I reached my readers through email marketing, social media, and events such as book fairs and book conferences.

Sometimes, even with the best laid plans, things may not go your way. But even in that, as a Faithful Entrepreneur, you have a secret weapon… prayer. Go to your heavenly Father and ask Him for direction. Ask God to lead you in the path that will bring you success. Then keep working, keep moving, and soon you will see God stepping in on your behalf.

6

MULTIPLE STREAMS OF INCOME

In business there will be plentiful times and lean times. No one questions their business ideas when the money is flowing like water. However, if the business doesn't have sufficient buffers you will not only question your business, you may have to put up a 'Business Closing' sign.

The buffer you will need is something called multiple streams of income. It doesn't matter what business you are in, you will need to find multiple ways to earn money from your business. Let's take my business model and dissect it. My business is writing.

When I began writing novels, I made sure that I would be able to earn money in multiple ways on the books that I wrote.

*Direct sales - My direct sales occurred a lot more during my early years when I was introducing myself to readers. I traveled all over the country paying for vendor tables at book fairs and at military bases. I would then sell my books directly to readers as they walked by my table.

*Online sales - I use PayPal or Square to accept online payments for books that I sell to consumers who want an autographed copy of one of my books. I also use Amazon, Barnes & Noble and several other online bookstores to sell my print books.

*Distributor sales - If you are an author like me, you'll want to have your books available in bookstores like Barnes & Noble and the like. To do this you'll need to work with distributors like Ingram or Baker & Taylor. These distributors will take a hefty percentage, something like 60% because they will also have to give a discount to the bookstore in order to get your book in the store.

*Publishers - During my years as a published author I have self-published and worked with publishers to get my books out to the public. To date I have worked with (4) publishers as a means of multiple streams of income.

*Speaking engagements - Depending on the type of business you are in, you can gain new clients/customers and a nice speaking fee from speaking engagements. How did I receive speaking engagements paying me as high as $2,000 for an hour speech? (Note: I have never charged anyone a specific amount. I like to stay within an organizations budget, so I have always stated that my speaking fee is anywhere from $350-$2,000 based on the budget. Then I stipulate that I must be allowed to sell my books afterwards).

You will set up your speaker fee in the manner that you are most comfortable. I have always trusted that God would move mightily, and I would be able to sell enough books to get me to my ultimate goal amount… but that's just me.

*Ebook sales - This stream of income was not even a possibility for me until late 2010. And in truth, it became my biggest source of income, earning me tens of thousands of dollars per month. But that never would have happened if I had not been doing direct, online, distributor, and publisher sales all those other years. Because of the work I had put in early on, once ebook sales became a reality, my audience was there and ready to support my new stream of income.

*Audio book sales - I have produced several audio books of some of the books that I have written. Audible Books now makes it possible for authors to hire voice artists to create an audio version of your book.

As a practice, I incorporate multiple streams of income wherever possible. But those streams always seem to come from writing. Why is that? Because writing is my passion; it is the gift God gave me, and He has allowed me to make a living from this gift. Let's discuss other ways I have used multiple streams of income. Besides the books that I write, I have produced (4) anthologies. Other writers pay to be a part of the anthologies that I produce and then they receive books that they can sell in order to make their money back…

so in my opinion, it is a win-win situation. I've done stage plays, and now I host an annual retreat. The Christian Book Lover's Retreat (CBLR) combines my two loves: being a Christian and books. Our tagline is: Faith. Fun. Fellowship… and a whole lot of books.

*Anthologies

*Stage Plays

*Christian Book Lover's Retreat

If you are keeping count, I just introduced to you (10) ways I use multiple streams of income to keep my business alive and thriving. I give all glory to God that I have been able to make a living doing what I love by creating multiple streams of income. I pray that this section has inspired you to come up with ways in which you can use multiple streams of income to grow your business.

Name at least seven ways of earning money from (1) product/ service that you offer:

1 _____

_____

2 _____

_____

3 _____

_____

4 _____

_____

5 _____

_____

6 _____

_____

7 _____

_____

Now that you have figured out the different ways you can earn money in your business, put a strategy together to make those things happen. If you are a writer like me, you might be interested in my special report, *Secrets to Earning Six Figures... And More As a Self-Publisher*. This special report is available on amazon.com, and it provides further information on each of the streams of income I discussed in this chapter. I provide names of suppliers and companies you will want to do business with to further your writing career. But since this book is not just about writers, but anyone who is a Faithful Entrepreneur, I will not bore you with those details here. I am providing the link, if you'd like to review the easy read, quick guide to self-publishing and making money: http://bit.ly/SecretToSixFigures

For other occupations, my advice is to do your research. Talk with others who are in the same field and ask them how they deal with multiple streams of income. Understanding this principle will allow you to stay in business when others drop out. So, do your research and find every possible avenue to bring income into your business.

7

FAITH FOR THE LEAN TIMES

Times were good. I had been a full-time, self-employed writer for over a decade with about 30 books in print and ebook. I had witnessed God increase my income to the point where I was earning hundreds of thousands of dollars each year. I bought the Lexus SUV that I'd always wanted. Owned a home in Ohio and another home in Charlotte. Paid for numerous vacations and cruises for my family. I was doing good and life was good. Then the bottom fell out.

As my grandson has told me, I'm a spender. So, I wasn't prepared for the car accident that left me with a broken ankle, months away from writing because the surgeries caused too much pain to work. I spent months healing, and learning to walk again... believe me, breaking an ankle is no small thing. Nor was I prepared for all the hospital bills that followed. To make matter's worse, at the same time I was going through this, the renter I had for my Ohio home stopped paying her rent. When she moved out, she left the house with tens of thousands of dollars of damage.

Keep in mind that I had spent over ten thousand dollars just two years prior on repairs and updates for that home before renting it out to anyone. During this time, ebook sales slowed down tremendously. I wasn't bringing in the type of money that I had once made, so I couldn't just make all of the issues go away. So, what did I do... again, this is where FAITH comes in. The situation was stressing me, and causing me to feel ill at times, but I kept praying, asking God to show me what needed to be done.

I had an excellent credit rating and didn't want to lose that. But I also didn't want to lose the home I owned in Charlotte, because I lived in this home. After running the numbers, I realized that even after owning the house in Ohio for fifteen years, I was upside down on that house because the home prices fell and had not recovered. So, even if I found the money to fix the issues with that house, I would still be at a loss, because if I sold the house I would have to bring about $20,000 to closing.

Seeing those numbers took the stress away. I informed the bank that I would be giving the house back to them and deal with the fall out. I thought that having such a hit to my credit score would make it hard for me to do business and obtain loans if the business needed it. But My God never sleeps nor slumbers when it comes to taking care of me.

Remember: Faith is the substance of things hoped for, the evidence of things not seen. So, even when things are going bad, or you are experiencing lean times, this is when your faith must be at its highest. You must continue to believe that God is on your side and that God has your best interests at heart.

Remember those so-called friends of Job who told him that he must have sinned in order to be dealing with such awful things in his life. But Job was not persuaded by the negativity of those who kicked him while he was down. All of his life he had trusted God, and in this too, he decided that he would trust God and hold onto his shield of faith... and God returned to Job everything he had lost.

As I kept trusting God through my own wilderness experience (which was nothing compared to what Job went through), God brought me out. But He didn't just bring me out financially, God also answered another prayer that had been on my list for so long that, at times, I wondered if it would ever happen. Here's how it all went down...

I'm at home recovering from my broken ankle and feeling sorry for myself because I wasn't able to travel as much as I used to. Remember, traveling had always been one of my streams of income because I would travel to events and sell my books. Being able to do this would have helped my cash flow problems. But I couldn't get on the road and drive, not even after my ankle was strong enough, because I started having panic attacks on the highway. This was strange to me because my accident happened on a neighborhood street.

I kept praying, asking God to get my mind back on writing so that I could write my next book and earn a living. One day it happened, God gave me a new series, *The Family Business Series*, and I began writing again. But it wasn't just that I was finally able to write, but my readers were there to purchase the books, and I am forever thankful for that.

However, I still wanted to be able to connect with my readers as I had been able to do when I traveled from city to city, from this event to the next event. One day I mentioned to my daughter that I missed seeing my readers and she said to me, why don't you do a book event that will bring them to Charlotte... and the Christian Book Lover's Retreat was born.

I wasn't sure if I could get the funding for some of the things I needed to do in order to pull this kind of retreat together. But low and behold God had already went before me and worked that out. Because of the business that I had done with PayPal for over a decade, they knew that my business was sound, and they gleefully loaned me money and I didn't even have to pay interest on it. The money from PayPal was paid back within months as attendees began signing up for the first-ever Christian Book Lover's Retreat.

The first retreat occurred in 2016. It is now 2018, and the retreat continues to grow with hundreds of readers and writers attending the retreat. I am believing God for a thousand attendees each year at the retreat. When He will manifest those numbers, I cannot tell you, but I wait patiently for Him to do His work.

And slowly but surely, God even took away the panic attacks, and I started traveling again. I am now booking speaking engagements and am very happy to be doing so. I am not a speaker when it comes to preaching and writing sermons, but no one is better at telling my story than I am. I also love encouraging God's people to rise up and live the life He planned for them. I have been invited to speak at Women's ministries and book events all over the country and I do my best to share what God put on my heart.

I have said on numerous occasions that outside of the year my mother passed away, which really threw me for a loop, 2015 was the worst year of my adult life. It seemed that everywhere I turned something went wrong, starting with that broken ankle, my grandmother passing away and going through all that drama with my rental property in Ohio.

But out of those ashes, God created something beautiful and gave me so many reasons to smile again. First, the creation of the Christian Book Lover's Retreat, then I began writing again, thus the Family Business series, and finally, after praying for a husband for years and trusting God with the outcome, He finally sent the love of my life. And even with that, God showed me that He was the one in control of me and if I just paid attention to the clues, I would see the manifestation of my prayers.

This is a total side note, but I tell this story so you can see and believe how faith and trust in God works... the number one item on my prayer list when it came to a husband was that he be saved and love the Lord.

One month after I gave my life to God, I was serving as a greeter at a women's conference my church hosted at Stuffers (that was the name of the hotel back then. I believe it is the Crown Plaza now). A man who worked for this hotel approached me. He was very polite and asked me out on a date. I was also polite to him, but at the same time I informed him that I do not date unsaved men.

His response, "What church do you attend?" I told him the name of my church and thought nothing else about it. The next day was Sunday, and low and behold this man showed up at the church. I said hello, but basically ignored him after that, because I had prayed for a saved man and I could tell that he had not given his life to the Lord, as yet.

He eventually gave his life to the Lord and we were friendly, but our lives went in different directions. Twenty years later, still living for the Lord and now an ordained minister, this man (David) contacted me and asked me out again. Of course, I said yes, and the rest is history. You may be thinking that God has forgotten you and your dreams. But, I tell you to look at the situation again. Maybe

God has sent the answer to your prayer, but it wasn't packaged the way you thought it would be, so you are still sitting there without the husband you desire… without the business you're supposed to be thriving in… without the ministry you're supposed to be serving God's people in.

Your wilderness situation may be of your own making, but guess what, God will still step in and turn it around for your good. I know the God I serve, because He has shown Himself mightily to me too many times for me to doubt Him. When things aren't going the way I need them to, I don't stress out, I turn the situation over to God in prayer and I keep moving forward.

In good times and bad, you must always do as the Bible instructs in Ephesians 6:11-18

11 Put on the whole armor of God, that ye may be able to stand against the wiles of the devil.
12 For we wrestle not against flesh and blood, but against principalities, against powers, against the rulers of the darkness of this world, against spiritual wickedness in high places.
13 Wherefore take unto you the whole armor of God, that ye may be able to withstand in the evil day, and having done all, to stand.
14 Stand therefore, having your loins girt about with truth, and having on the breastplate of righteousness;
15 And your feet shod with the preparation of the gospel of peace;
16 Above all, taking the shield of faith, wherewith ye shall be able to quench all the fiery darts of the wicked.
17 And take the helmet of salvation, and the sword of the Spirit, which is the word of God:

18 Praying always with all prayer and supplication in the Spirit, and watching thereunto with all perseverance and supplication for all saints;

When you put on the whole armor of God, you will be able to get through the lean times with your faith in God, which then allows Him to work a miracle on your behalf. I tell you the truth, I'd rather have Jesus than all the silver and gold in the land. Because as long as I hold onto my faith, I know that if one business flops, God will help me to create another business that will propel me further than I ever imagined I could go in the first place. So, stand fast in your faith. Let nothing stop you from believing that God has your best interests at heart and that He wants to prosper you and give you success in your business endeavors, as well as your spiritual life. Let's go get it!

8

SETTING UP YOUR BUSINESS WITH GOD IN MIND

I purposely put this chapter at to the back of the book because I wanted to talk to you about faith as it relates to any business that you may run before we set the business up. The reason... now I'm going to suggest that you consider naming your business something that lets the world know where you stand. And not just the world, I want YOU to always remember who you are in Christ and who you belong to as you do business in this wicked world.

The name of my business is Praise Unlimited Enterprises. So, to me that means, no matter what I do, it must be something that brings praise to the Lord. As a Faithful Entrepreneur, you will come into contact with many people who are shady in business dealings. They believe to get ahead, they have to step on others. They back bite and down other people's businesses in order to lift their business up, but that should never be said of you. When you are in business because you believe that what you are doing will further the cause of Christ, then the way you act and respond in business dealings must also show the love of Christ.

Why does the way you treat people matter? Because our job as Christians is to always be ready to give an answer for the hope that lies within us. If you are corrupt in your business dealings, or mistreat the people you come in contact with, do you really believe that they will be able to receive a word from God from you? Or will that person say, 'if this is how Christians act, then I don't want any part of the God they serve'?

Remember, our end goal is to hear the Lord say, "Well done My good and faithful servant." So, watch how you treat people if you call yourself a Faithful Entrepreneur. Furthermore, and this is just my opinion so do with it what you will, but I believe that a Faithful Entrepreneur furthers the cause of Christ by naming their business something that relates to Christiandom. Think about it, anyone reading the name of your business will know where you stand. But not only that, we don't know what God will use to plant or water a seed he has already placed in another.

What if someone who God is wooing into His loving arms sees a truck every day that drives down her street with the words, Praise Unlimited, or For the Love of Christ Ministry, or Heavenly Cookies… you get the drift. One day someone witnesses to her, and her mind drifts back to that truck, and finally she is ready to give Jesus a try. You had no idea that it was the name of your business that stayed on this woman's mind, but God knows, and your faithfulness puts a smile on His face.

Setting Up The Business:

The first thing you'll need to do is come up with a name for your company. Then you will need to incorporate your business. There are four most used types of business you'll want to consider: LLC, S Corp, C Corp, or nonprofit. Let's go over these so you can make a decision:

Limited Liability Company or LLC

LLCs shield the owners, who are called members, from being personally liable for actions of the company. LLCs also provide flexibility in management and allow the profits and losses of the business to pass through to its owners, as they are reported on their personal tax returns. Pass-through taxation is one of the reasons why LLCs are significantly easier to run compared to a corporation.

Why do some choose an LLC

If you want to avoid personal risks of lawsuits that may arise from your business, then you should consider forming an LLC. Basically, having an LLC means if you are sued, the person can only come after your business assets, not your personal assets such as your home.

S Corp

The S corporation business type comes with an advantage: it has the limited liability of a corporation, but without the "double taxation" of income passed through to the shareholders. Prior to the acceptance of the LLC, the S corporation was the best vehicle to shield the owners while avoiding double taxation. The S corporation lets a business owner use the business losses—such as losses incurred during the startup of a business —on their personal returns as deductions. S corporations can also provide savings for their owners on self-employment or Social Security/Medicare taxes, along with the FICA (Federal Insurance Contributions Act) tax.

Why do some choose an S corporation?

An S corporation allows the owners to offset non-business income with losses from the business, unlike a C corporation which is a completely separate tax entity. When compared to an LLC, the S corporation enables an owner to characterize a portion of income as "dividend," rather than "earnings" that are subject to employment taxes.

C Corp

C corporations are actually the most common business type. The C Corporation offers more flexibility than S corporations because you can have more owners/shareholders with a piece of the business. This type of business also allows the owner to deduct employee benefits. For this reason, C corporations are preferred by upstart businesses.

Why do some choose an C corporation?

The flexibility with the number of owners is the best reason for this type of corporation. Also, the owners can hold different types of stock interests (such as preferred versus common stock.) Note: venture capitalists choose C corporations when they offer funding to a business. A C corporation can also retain and accumulate earnings (within reasonable limits) from year to year.

Non-Profit

A nonprofit corporation is one that is formed for other reasons than making a profit. Examples of nonprofits include churches and hospitals. Forming a nonprofit company can help you avoid personal liability for the debts of your company. The primary advantage to nonprofit companies is that the company will be able to receive both private and public grants.

Why form a non-profit?

You do not have to incorporate your nonprofit venture, but it lends more credibility to the company if you do. Also, in order to become tax-exempt, you must incorporate and also file Form 1023 with the Internal Revenue Service. A few states require a separate filing for state tax-exempt status as well.

What does it mean to incorporate?

Incorporating a business means turning your dream or vision into a company formally recognized by your state as a business. When a company incorporates, it is now its own legal business structure set apart from the individuals who founded the business. Your business transactions are now separate from your personal transactions. Contact their local Small Business Association or SCORE office if you need assistance in deciding how to incorporate your business or any advice in starting a business.

Once you have decided on a name, and what type of business you will incorporate as, you will then need to contact the Secretary of State to incorporate your business. You'll need The Articles of Incorporation Form. The fee for filing this form in my state is $125. Below you will find a link to the Secretary of State of NC. This link will provide you with all the information needed to file The Articles of Incorporation. But if you do not live in North Carolina, please go to the website for the Secretary of State where you live and locate the Articles of Incorporation Form. However, the links below may give you an idea of where to look on your state's website:

https://www.secretary.state.nc.us/corporations/pdf/ BusinessCorporation.pdf

How to **obtain the articles of incorporation application form.**

- Log onto the North Carolina Secretary of State's website at www.secretary.state.nc.us/corporations.
- Click on the link for "Business Corporations" under the heading "Print Corporation Forms."
- Download the articles of incorporation form.

Once your business has been incorporated, you will receive an EIN (Employer Identification Number). You will be able to use this EIN number to file taxes for your business. Remember, businesses receive more tax deductions than individuals, so discuss the benefits of incorporating with a tax professional.

9

FAITHFUL ENTREPRENEURS GIVE BACK

"Honor the Lord with your wealth, with the first fruits of your crops; then your barns will be filled to overflowing, and your vats will brim over with new wine." ~Proverbs 3:9-10

I can clearly remember calling my pastor the week after I gave my life to the Lord. This tithing thing was a new concept to me, but when I fell in love with Jesus I was all in, so if I had to give 10% of my income, then so be it. But I didn't know whether that 10% should be given off the before tax income I received or after taxes. In my mind it should be after taxes, because, come on, that's all I get to spend, the government took the rest.

But Pastor Willie E. Mitchell explained to me that he taught that tithes should be given off of the gross income. This conversation occurred almost twenty-five years ago, so I don't remember his exact words, but it had something to do with bringing God the spoils from the fatted calf rather than a sickly calf. When I hung up the phone I realized something... my take home income was like a sickly calf, because I wasn't earning much in those days.

I wanted to give God my best so even though I was a single parent, earning about nine dollars an hour at that time, I decided to trust the Lord. I began paying my tithes, not on the net but on the gross. And now I'm going to tell you what God did for me after making that faithful decision to give Him my best.

I was working at a Fortune 500 company, so possibilities were endless, but I never noticed those possibilities until God opened my eyes. Within a year, I received a promotion to team leader. I then went back to college. It took only three years for me to earn my bachelor's degree. But by that time, I had already been promoted to supervisor over my department. Here's the thing about that... just before I gave my life to God, the director of that department was threatening to fire me for excessive telephone usage. Not only that, I was in a department with women who had been hired into that department the same day it was formed. These women knew the job backwards and forwards, but God still elevated me over them. Why? Because I trusted Him to take my little and turn it into much.

The director of that department went from wanting to fire me to calling me his shining eagle, because I became one of the most productive employees in that department, and all because of my decision to give God my best. I want God to have my best in tithes, my work, and how I treat others, and God has honored me for the heart that I have towards Him… I truly believe that. And just to show off, God allowed me to be promoted on that job once again. This time, I received a position for which I had no experience. By the time I left that company to begin my writing career, I was a long way from $9 an hour, and I give all glory to God. He and He alone has elevated me, simply because I decided to trust Him.

But here's the thing… can you keep on trusting Him? Can you be trusted with more? See, I proved that I could be trusted with more while working for Corporate America. I didn't think twice about giving the Lord what was due Him. Back then at my highest earning level in Corporate America, my tithes grew from $144 to $450 a month. If it wasn't for God, I would have still been earning the scraps that barely fed my daughter, so I gladly increased my tithes as my income increased.

Now let's fast forward as I take the time to be completely transparent with you. Some years later, after working my business and my plan, I became what I consider a successful writer with several books in print and ebooks. I was earning anywhere from ten, fifteen to twenty thousand a month. And instead of being so, so grateful to God as I had been before, I began to resent writing such big tithe checks. Let me be real with you, $450 a month in tithes is one thing, $1500 to $2000 is a whole nother-other. I remember saying to someone, that I felt bad about not wanting to write that check some months. I'll never forget what she said to me, "God could just reduce your earnings, then you won't have to pay so much in tithes. Would that help?"

No! I wanted to scream. No way did I want to go back to earning the money I had once been earning, so I kept paying my tithes. The difference was that paying my tithes in the beginning had been out of love, now it was more out of duty. So, when I moved out of town and no longer had a church home, I continued to pay my tithes to whatever church I was attending at that time. But there came a day when my heart showed its true colors.

I decided I would build a home. I'd never had a house built, and I felt that I deserved that. But here's the thing, I still owned a house in Ohio and the renter was shaky. I knew this, but I still wanted this big house in this exclusive neighborhood. To make the numbers work, I had to put down thirty thousand dollars on the house. So, I said to myself, "You can do this if you spend wisely for the next few months. You're not a member of that church you've been attending, so why are you paying tithes over there?" And just like that, my plan to defraud my savior was formed.

Not in a million years could you have ever convinced me that money would come between me and my God, whom I love so dearly. I'm thankful every day that He saved my soul and took my life from ashes to beauty. And my Lord allowed me to make that foolish mistake. I bought the house, watched them build it, took pictures of the progress and then my family and I moved in. I told you what happened next in the chapter, Faith or the Lean Times… I got into a car wreck, broke my ankle, totaled my car, couldn't work for several months, lost the house in Ohio, and on and on. I lost a lot, but I still have the home that I loved so much and built from the ground up. However, I truly believe that my lean times occurred because I stopped trusting God with my best, and decided to give Him that sickly calf.

But the God I serve is merciful, and He is full of grace. I have learned that it is better to give God your best and sit back and watch Him give you His best. I pay my tithes with gladness these days. I don't look at the amount and think about other things I could do with that money, because I have learned that things can change in a moment. Instead of writing a big tithe check, you'll be in church wishing you could write one. When God has been good to you, don't ever forget Him… don't watch the Joneses and think you deserve what they have. Be grateful for what God allows to come into your life and pray and ask Him for more, if that is what you desire. He's a good God. He will answer your prayers, if you let Him.

Tithes are very important for a Christian because this is where you demonstrate your faith, showing that you trust God to take care of you with the 90% leftover. And believe me when I tell you, I'm a living witness, He is well able. I don't know whether your pastor teaches paying tithes on the gross or the net, and I'm not here to judge which way you do it. I was only informing you about how I learned to pay tithes. But tithes are not the only way a Faithful Entrepreneur can or should give back. Let's look at James 2:14-26:

14 What *does it* profit, my brethren, if someone says he has faith but does not have works? Can faith save him? **15** If a brother or sister is naked and destitute of daily food, **16** and one of you says to them, "Depart in peace, be warmed and filled," but you do not give them the things which are needed for the body, what *does it* profit? **17** Thus also faith by itself, if it does not have works, is dead.

18 But someone will say, "You have faith, and I have works." Show me your faith without your[d] works, and I will show you my faith by my[e] works. **19** You believe that there is one God. You do well. Even the demons believe—and tremble! **20** But do you want to know, O foolish man, that faith without works is dead?[f] **21** Was not Abraham our father justified by works when he offered Isaac his son on the altar? **22** Do you see that faith was working together with his works, and by works faith was made perfect? **23** And the Scripture was fulfilled which says, "Abraham believed God, and it was accounted to him for righteousness."[g] And he was called the friend of God. **24** You see then that a man is justified by works, and not by faith only.

25 Likewise, was not Rahab the harlot also justified by works when she received the messengers and sent *them* out another way?

26 For as the body without the spirit is dead, so faith without works is dead also.

When I read these scriptures, it tells me that God wants action from me that demonstrates my faith in Him. One action is paying my tithes. Another action could be helping out at a homeless shelter or volunteering at church, because you took time away from work when you could be making money. Do you believe that God will reward you for doing something like that?

I am a private person. You won't find me on Facebook ranting about how somebody did me wrong or freely telling my business to others. And yet, I decided that if I was going to write this book, I would lay it out there… the good, bad, and not so pretty. Therefore, this book became my way of giving back. I truly want to see Christian entrepreneurs succeed in this world. I believe I have found the answer and it is trusting in Jesus and then working the plan. So, I have decided to take as many people as will go along on this faith journey with me.

How about it? Are you a Faithful Entrepreneur? Do you trust God with your life and your dreams? Do you believe that God can take you further than you can take yourself? Do you want to experience the hundred-fold blessing? I know I do and I'm believing Him for it. I wish I could see your face right now. I pray you have this look of excitement on your face as your understanding has been enlightened by reading this book.

I pray that you now know that God is no respecter of person. What He does for one, He will do for another. All God needs from you is the faith of a mustard seed. Give it to God and allow Him to grow it. Repeat this scripture: *Beloved I wish above all things that you prosper and be in good health even as your soul prospers*. Keep saying it until you believe and understand that YOU are the beloved God is talking about. As your faith grows, you'll be able to work the business that God has put in you from the foundation of the world, and then you will truly be doing the will of God. Can you see what I see? All of the Faithful Entrepreneurs out there bringing souls into the kingdom... oh how glorious it will be. Let's get started!

Thank you so much for reading the Faithful Entrepreneur. I wish you all the success in the world, so go after that dream or vision God gave you like it is the reason you were born. It is the thing you were meant to do after all, and no one will do it better that you because God is on your side. Remember, God needs as many warriors on the battlefield. So, take up your armor, fight the good fight of faith and make it happen! Many blessings to you.

Bonus Section

SCRIPTURES TO MEDITATE ON AS YOU BUILD YOUR BUSINESS

"Oh, that you would bless me and enlarge my territory! Let your hand be with me, and keep me from harm so that I will be free from pain."

~ 1 Chronicles 4:10

But as for you, be strong and do not give up, for your work will be rewarded.

~ 2 Chronicles 15:7

May he give you the desire of your heart and make all your plans succeed.

~ Psalm 20:4

But the plans of the Lord stand firm forever, the purposes of his heart through all generations.

~ Psalm 33:11

Delight yourself in the Lord, and he will give you the desires of your heart.

~ Psalm 37:4

It is better to take refuge in the Lord than to trust in humans.

~ Psalm 118:8

Unless the Lord builds the house, the builders labor in vain.

~ Psalm 127:1

Trust in the LORD with all your heart, And do not lean on your own understanding. In all your ways acknowledge Him, And He will make your paths straight.

~ Proverbs 3:5-6

Without consultation, plans are frustrated, but with many counselors they succeed.

~ Proverbs 15:22

Commit to the Lord whatever you do, and he will establish your plans.

~ Proverbs 16:3

In their hearts humans plan their course, but the LORD establishes their steps.

~ Proverbs 16:9

Many are the plans in a person's heart, but it is the Lord's purpose that prevails.

~ Proverbs 19:21

The plans of the diligent lead surely to abundance.

~ Proverbs 21:5

Where there is no vision, the people are unrestrained, but happy is he who keeps the law.

~ Proverbs 29:18

But the noble make noble plans, and by noble deeds they stand.

~ Isaiah 32:8

But they that wait upon the LORD shall renew [their] strength; they shall mount up with wings as eagles; they shall run, and not be weary; [and] they shall walk, and not faint.

~ Isaiah 40:31

See, I am doing a new thing! Now it springs up; do you not perceive it? I am making a way in the wilderness and streams in the wasteland.

~ Isaiah 43:19

As the heavens are higher than the earth, so are my ways higher than your ways and my thoughts than your thoughts.

~ Isaiah 55:9

But blessed is the one who trusts in the Lord, whose confidence is in him.

~ Jeremiah 17:7

What does the Lord require of you but to do justice, and to love kindness, and to walk humbly with your God?

~ Micah 6:8

And the Lord answered me: "Write the vision; make it plain on tablets, so he may run who reads it. For still the vision awaits its appointed time; it hastens to the end—it will not lie. If it seems slow, wait for it; it will surely come; it will not delay.

~ Habakkuk 2:2-3

New Testament

Do not lay up for yourselves treasures on earth, where moth and rust destroy and where thieves break in and steal, but lay up for yourselves treasures in heaven, where neither moth nor rust destroys and where thieves do not break in and steal. For where your treasure is, there your heart will be also.

~ Matthew 6:19-21

But seek first the kingdom of God and his righteousness, and all these things will be added to you.

~ Matthew 6:33

Truly I tell you, if you have faith as small as a mustard seed, you can say to this mountain, 'Move from here to there,' and it will move. Nothing will be impossible for you.

~ Matthew 17:20

But Jesus looked at them and said, "With man this is impossible, but with God all things are possible.

~ Matthew 19:26

And whatever you ask in prayer, you will receive, if you have faith.

~ Matthew 21:22

Then Jesus explained: "My nourishment comes from doing the will of God, who sent me, and from finishing his work. Jesus said to them, "My food is to do the will of him who sent me and to accomplish his work.

~ John 4:34

And we know that for those who love God all things work together for good, for those who are called according to his purpose.

~ Romans 8:28

Do not be conformed to this world, but be transformed by the renewal of your mind, that by testing you may discern what is the will of God, what is good and acceptable and perfect.

~ Romans 12:2

Now to Him who is able to do far more abundantly beyond all that we ask or think, according to the power that works within us, to Him be the glory in the church and in Christ Jesus to all generations forever and ever. Amen.

~ Ephesians 3:20-21

I can do all things through him who strengthens me.

~ Philippians 4:13

Forgetting what lies behind and straining forward to what lies ahead, I press on toward the goal for the prize of the upward call of God in Christ Jesus.

~ Philippians 3:13-14

So do not throw away your confidence; it will be richly rewarded.

You need to persevere so that when you have done the will of God,

you will receive what he has promised.

~ Hebrews 10:35-36

Therefore, since we are surrounded by so great a cloud of witnesses,

let us also lay aside every weight, and sin which clings so closely,

and let us run with endurance the race that is set before us, looking

to Jesus, the founder and perfecter of our faith, who for the joy that

was set before him endured the cross, despising the shame, and is

seated at the right hand of the throne of God. Consider him who

endured from sinners such hostility against himself, so that you may

not grow weary or fainthearted.

~ Hebrews 12:1-3

You do not even know what will happen tomorrow. What is your life? You are a mist that appears for a little while and then vanishes. Instead, you ought to say, 'If it is the Lord's will, we will live and do this or that.'

~ James 4:13-15

The end of Book 1

Stay tuned for Book 2, Entrepreneur Girl coming in February

2019

Don't forget to join my mailing list:

http://vanessamiller.com/events/join-mailing-list/

Join me on Facebook: https://www.facebook.com/groups/

77899021863/

Join the Faithful Entrepreneur's Club: fb.me/

faithfulentrepreneursclub

Join me on Twitter: https://www.twitter.com/vanessamiller01

Other Business Books by Vanessa

Faithful Entrepreneur Workbook/Planner

Secrets to Earning Six Figures… And more as a Self-Publisher

http://bit.ly/SecretToSixFigures

About the Author

Vanessa Miller is a best-selling author, Entrepreneur, playwright, and motivational speaker. She started writing as a child, spending countless hours either reading or writing poetry, short stories, stage plays, and novels. Vanessa's creative endeavors took on new meaning in1994 when she became a Christian. Since then, her writing has been centered on themes of redemption, often focusing on characters facing multi-dimensional struggles.

Vanessa's novels have received rave reviews, with several appearing on *Essence Magazine's* Bestseller's List. Miller's work has receiving numerous awards, including "Best Christian Fiction Mahogany Award" and the "Red Rose Award for Excellence in Christian Fiction." Miller graduated from Capital University with a degree in Organizational Communication. She is an ordained minister in her church, explaining, "God has called me to minister to readers and to help them rediscover their place with the Lord."

She has worked with numerous publishers: Urban Christian, Kimani Romance, Abingdon Press and Whitaker House. She is currently Indy published through Praise Unlimited enterprises and working on the Family Business Series.

In 2016, Vanessa launched the Christian Book Lover's Retreat in an effort to bring readers and authors of Christian fiction together in an environment that's all about Faith, Fun & Fellowship. To learn more about Vanessa, please visit her website: www.vanessamiller.com. If you would like to know more about the Christian Book Lover's Retreat that is currently held in Charlotte, NC during the last week in October, you can visit: http://www.christianbookloversretreat.com/index.html

If you would like to book Vanessa to speak at your women's conference, retreat, or book event email your request to: vmiller-01@earthlink.net.

Don't forget to join my mailing list:

http://vanessamiller.com/events/join-mailing-list/

Join me on Facebook: https://www.facebook.com/groups/

77899021863/

Join me on Twitter: https://www.twitter.com/vanessamiller01

Order Form

Item	Qty	Cost	Total
Faithful Entrepreneur		$15.99	
Entrepreneur Girl (rel. date Feb. 2019)		$15.99	
Faithful Entrepreneur Workbook/Planner		$19.99	
Faithful t-shirt (Small - XL)		$15.00	
Faithful t-shirt (2X-3X)		$18.00	
Shipping/Handling		$6.99	
-Total			

Order Information:

Name: _____

Address: _____

Email: _____ Phone: _____

Master Card / Visa / Paypal

CC#: _____ Exp Date: _____

(3) digit Security Code: _____

To Pay by Check or Money Order:

Mail Check to: Vanessa Miller

13000 S. Tryon Street * Suite F-331

Charlotte, NC 28278